LISTENING TO AFRICA

OTHER POETRY COLLECTIONS BY DIANA M. RAAB

The Guilt Gene (2009)
Dear Anaïs: My Life in Poems for You (2008)
My Muse Undresses Me (2007)

Listening to Africa

Poems by Diana M. Raab

Antrim House
Simsbury, Connecticut

Copyright © 2012 by Diana M. Raab

Except for short selections reprinted for purposes of
book review, all reproduction rights are reserved.
Requests for permission to replicate should
be addressed to the publisher.

Library of Congress Control Number: 2012930674

ISBN: 978-1-936482-18-4

First Edition, 2012

Photographs and sketches by Simon and Rachel Raab

Cover art, "Tribal Design," by Jim Edmon
iStock Vectors/Getty Images

Book Design by Rennie McQuilkin

Antrim House
860.217.0023
AntrimHouse@comcast.net
www.AntrimHouseBooks.com
21 Goodrich Road, Simsbury, CT 06070

This book is dedicated to my family,
Simon, Rachel, Regine and Joshua
for their boundless love, curiosity and enthusiasm

Acknowledgements

Grateful acknowledgement to the editors and staff of the following publications, where a few of the poems in this volume first appeared, sometimes in earlier versions:

Jet Fuel Review: "Bush Solace," "Visiting This New Continent" (Spring, 2011)

Snail Mail Review: "I'm Wondering" (February, 2011)

* * * * *

My heartfelt gratitude goes to all of my friends, family and colleagues who provide me with their love and inspiration to write poetry.

There are a few people I would like to personally thank for nurturing my poetic life:

Tristine Rainer, who inspired me to pull together this collection. Visiting Africa was one of her childhood dreams, but she now believes that she will never visit and that "armchair travel would be the next best choice."

Thomas Steinbeck, for his friendship and our wonderful "coffee happy hours," and for relentlessly encouraging the "poet in me"; Perie Longo, whose positive attitude, sense of humor, and moral support have helped me in so many ways; Kim Stafford, who has always believed in my projects; Phillip Lopate for his friendship and enthusiasm; David Starkey for his genuine camaraderie and support; Susan Wooldridge for her kindness and love; and all the poets I have been blessed to meet over the years.

Maggie Lang for her personal assistance.

And a special *merci* to Molly Peacock, who has been my shining light throughout this project and has motivated me with her persistent enthusiasm and suggestions that have helped bring this project to fruition. I will be forever thankful she is in my life.

My publisher, Rennie McQuilkin, for his kindness and for believing in this project.

And of course, my deepest gratitude to Simon and Rachel Raab for the wonderful photographs and sketches in this collection.

Table of Contents

EPIGRAPHS / ix

I. EARLY THOUGHTS

48-Hour Travel / 5
Pulled to Africa / 7
Amplified Melancholy / 8
Luggage Limits / 9
Jo-Berg / 10
Christmas Woes / 12

II. NAMIBIA

Nonchalant Pilot / 15
Suspended in a Telescope / 16
Disease Dance / 17
Digestive Paranoia / 18
The Scent of Death / 19
Balloon Rides / 21
All I Want Is a Thesaurus / 23
Escape / 24

III. BOTSWANA

Visiting This New Continent / 27
Bush Solace / 28
The Little Things / 29
King Pride / 31
Your Camera / 32
Lost / 33
Our Mission / 35
Creatures / 36
Their Flu / 37

IV. ZIMBABWE

I'm Wondering / 41
Camp Lessons / 42
Hippos / 43
The Speckled One / 45
Baobab Trees and Hyenas / 46
The Gentlest Animal / 48
Mischievous Monkeys / 50
The Circle / 53
Dung Beetles / 54
Tse Tse Paradise / 55
Elephant Cluster / 56
In Wonder / 58
The Market Visit / 59
Poverty / 60
No Gala / 61
The Last Evening of 2008 in Africa / 63
Departure Morning / 64
Trip Summary / 66

ABOUT THE AUTHOR / 69

ABOUT THE BOOK / 70

"I dream of the realization of the unity of Africa, whereby its leaders combine in their efforts to solve the problems of this continent. I dream of our vast deserts, of our forests, of all our great wilderness."

– Nelson Mandela

Listen – listen – across the land called Africa –
For the birds are singing here
The roar of the lioness – the whine of her cubs
The cry of the vultures – ever, ever circling there –

Oh – see for miles
No tangled web of wires
Endless horizons spread
No polluted mists – a view that will never tire ….

– Dorothy M. Center

I. Early Thoughts

48-Hour Travel

Should you decide
to take a safari here

you might want to consider
packing some meager comforts of home,

even though they will do little
to protect you from

such haunting newness.
But still, take a two-day supply of patience,

ear plugs, sleeping pills, a few good books,
a thick journal and a pound of prevention,

the comprehensive pill bag
with compartments for each ail.

If you plan on foreign intimacy,
don't rely on public bathrooms

to supply your protection—
be prepared with your own custom size.

For game rides, snatch volumes
of insect repellant and sunscreen

and a wrinkled ribbed hat,
to shield your neck

from the last blow
of the jungle's sunset

in this place which will
remind you of the reason for living.

Pulled to Africa

Half way through
my own century and perched
on my west coast suburban stoop,
I ponder my pull to Africa,

yanked from crispy white sheets
to musty humid canvas tents
where we will lay our heads to rest.

I welcome the change—the animal chatter,
excrement scents, people happy with so little
as I reflect upon memories
of my own troubled adolescence

which tore me from elusive dreams
and those within grandma's crystal ball—
her knowing all that was good for me
as I now know what is good for my kids

and how this visit will leave a trail of imprints
on my three grown metropolitan children
who will always remember this odyssey
into the deepest nights of Africa.

Amplified Melancholy

You might ask me to explain
this season's melancholy
slipping through my veins

and all I can tell you is that
on the tenth anniversary of dad's
passing, the doctors removed

my right breast and five years later
stabbed by a second diagnosis,
bone marrow malignancy,

no cure, just treatment—
the holiday lights sharpened.
Past dripping menorah candles,

I step onto African soil
with dreams of leaving
my own cells buried there

merging with a history
of African fights for survival,
even as I know there's no way,

except through magical dreams,
to leave behind what haunts me:
the healthy bones dad once bestowed.

Luggage Limits

Our pre-travel papers paint
reminders of a 39-pound luggage limit
(photos of bags slung
beneath tiny aircrafts

lifting us between
canvas-covered camps
past slinking hyenas

who hide food
for their young.)
So we travelers ponder

how to jam safari garb
into the prescribed suitcase size.
Is something wrong

with this picture,
this imbalance of sensibilities?—
how we have so much and they so little,

as we wedge all life's
eventualities between
the layers of transparent Ziplocs

then into compartments of Cessnas
which move our family of five
from country to country

over the vast emptiness
of this continent,
piggy-backed with faint hopes
of a faraway return.

Jo-Berg

We land into every traveler's nightmare—
luggage lost on foreign terrain, a suitcase

full with foreign fear and camera gear
as my own mind explodes

with thoughts nestled
between layers of lies

shared by aloof airline agents.
We wait inside our personal tour van,

noses pressed to its bullet proof
sliding glass windows, as I shiver

with anxiety of a potential breakdown
amidst rows of abandoned tin huts,

random public bathrooms
littered with flotsam of intimacy

and people wandering aimlessly.
Who can feel safe here?

They hold tight to endless dreams
in contrast to our familiar neon of home.

We seize our baggage, and they carry
their own truths upon their sun-struck faces.

Christmas Woes

The scent of Christmas
litters its sadness,
as it signals the time
of my dear father's passing
reminding me

how sad memories
stick to holidays
like ink smudges on
clean sheets of paper.
My heart feels stepped upon,

this crushing sensation
on the same beating muscle
inherited from my dad
with all its plaques of love,
as I press on in his footsteps

in the hope that he watches down
on my dreams postponed
during this painful
month of December.
How to disarm this month's power

with its sorrowful sun-beaten soil?
I climb the stairs one step at a time
uncovering this mysterious continent
with the same shape of a hand gun.

II. Namibia

Nonchalant Pilot

to Namibia

All set for take off, we huddle
under the thatched hut settled

onto the landing strip
in the heart of vast nowhere—

while our pilot paces his gravel runway,
and ground crew crush and push

our bags beneath this five-seater.
The door slams shut, and my lung pockets

swell with fear while the plane jitters
as in an epileptic fit. There is no briefing,

nor emergency instructions as we lift off
this red desert's crisp morning

and I pivot my head towards our nonchalant pilot
to pose a leisurely *what if* question,

as he cocks his head towards me and points
to the tri-fold instructions in the back-seat pocket,

tucked behind the wrinkled puke bag.
I stop to think that maybe

the plane is not as old as it smells
with empty ashtrays about

every inch of its perimeter as we look
at that now-abandoned thatched hut.

Suspended in a Telescope

in Namibia

After dinner we are invited
onto a distant dark rooftop
to peek through a telescope glancing
towards shiny clusters of galaxies
like the clusters of malignancies
in my own bone marrow.

We imagine a planet
embraced by astronomers
who sleep in faraway lands
under the spell of this magical horizon.

Those planets hold so many untouched corners,
never layered with human scars,
tears, or horror stories
as I sit on my own pinnacle,

eyes glued to the aperture
of this modern lens
to grasp dreams of a future
I most certainly will never live to see.

Disease Dance

While traveling this continent,
my safari pants' pockets
brim with Western remedies

to fend off threatened diseases
as germs and parasites conspire against me
within the waters and dense canopies.

We breathe and touch
strange sleeping and sucking ails,
unknown and unspeakable

on every fearsome occasion.
I reach down for the disinfectant
but do not want to touch the spot

laden with lurking dangers.
Under my breath I give thanks
to all the scientists who stand single file

awaiting kudos for their
germ-killing chemicals
nestled between me and the fatal demons.

Digestive Paranoia

All drinks and foods
echo travelogue warnings,

specified by tropical disease doctors
written with daunting stories

of the perils of lifelong parasites
and flat admonishments

about this disease-infested land.
I reflect upon the Aztecs and Indians

decimated by steel and germs
and I fear the revenge of the aborigines

passed out invisibly during handshakes,
while my latent cancer cells

which I carry in my mind and marrow,
must never be awakened

under the stars of this dark continent.
I slip through my day

and suckle from sealed bottles
with an ongoing digestive paranoia.

The Scent of Death

permeates this place
as my eyes adjust to a darkness
amidst whimpering humans,

naked children who sport
only skin and bones,
even though healthy bones.

If they had my disease,
death would enter quickly.
The medical care makes

a Westerner cringe—
no tablets, IV drops or doctors,
just bribes for wellness.

The forces of life and death
are at play like the day I found
my grandmother dead in her bed—

overdosed on sleeping pills.
Poverty flashes here,
hunger and disease unite

under broken street lights
and roadside huts.
This is their way of life,

and all I can think of is how
my family's love will heal me
and bring me back home

to my schooled doctors
and treatments which will save me
unlike the babies on these streets.

Balloon Rides

The Crocodile Dundee Congo Frenchman
prepares to lift us into the billowing sac of color
when suddenly hot gas explodes.

We sit inside horizontal bunk bed cradles
and embrace the slow, teetering lift-off.
There is a slight drag along stone

and then the diverging of two universes.
My family and I cradled under hot air and nylon—
delicate and suspended in imminent death.

Our expressions calm and entranced
and completely surrendered to
the physics of buoyancy.

The Namibian sky
lingers clear and endless
over the lavender orange chain

of numbered sand dunes.
Barren and desolated plains ponder
the cool night's air that will soothe
the soon-to-be-scorched terrain.

We are snapped into silence, then comes the roar
of dragon breath and then silence again.
The purple scarred panorama lingers

beneath our slow descent through

crisscrossing air currents
and a slow lug along earth.

This endless desert
is scarred by our cradle's comic crash
followed by grand finale festivities

culminating with champagne bottle
opened by Dundee's machete,
the sky a little less lavender than when we took off.

All I Want Is a Thesaurus

The first line of a poem just arrived
on the pages of my lean leather notebook
which balances on the ledge

of this mountaintop rock,
while an unknown word flutters
through the crevices of my aged brain.

I do not know its definition,
or the number of its letters.
All I know is it is the one I need right here,

right now, for this poem's progression.
Futile shuffles through the files of my mind
deliver only blank pages.

Nearby birds offer little help,
just platters of twigs
for their own private nest.

I swing my eyes to stare at imaginary stars
as if this remote land could meet my request
and like a little girl the day before Christmas,

I make a wish that one will
drop me a gift, wrapped
in crinkly silver paper and a flawless bow

hugging the covers of a crisp new thesaurus
to remind me of the world I left
and the journals deposited on my library shelves.

Escape

Today has been long
and the hot sun has finally
found its way home to its horizon.

I look into the distance and pray for a pause
before the African darkness strikes,
just so I can capture

more exotic photos and saturate
each sector of my brain
with this abundant beauty

for my moments of exhaustion,
after a day spent sighting beasts
and snatching hugs from my children

who will soon return to their own distant cities.
In the shared visitation of this foreign land,
we touch the reason for living at the end of each day.

III. Botswana

Visiting This New Continent

It is difficult to describe
how one feels being transported

into this world where
one feels like a stranger

in a strange land, delivered
into darkness by ten planes

in as many days. If
I squeeze my eyes closed

and blink them open again,
would it feel like

a moon landing
by a shattered spaceship?

The only difference
may be that gravity still digs

its claws into my psyche,
particularly when forced

to run from the male lion
eyeing me for dinner

in this deep African night!

Bush Solace

When left alone in an African jungle
realize that home
is different to everyone
and as much as you can pack
into one suitcase, it will never be enough
to erase the feeling of homesickness
knotted in your solar plexus.

The Little Things

On visits to remote lands
like Africa, little things
become big ones—

like morning wake-up calls
from charming frog princes,
freshly-brewed coffee,
a clean pair of underwear,

the warm sweater tossed
into the suitcase at the last moment,
the monkey who jumps

onto the tent's roof,
the nursing baby baboon,
elephant tracks during an afternoon stroll,
the deck of playing cards

in your carry-on, the iPhone
with downloaded Scrabble,
the lozenge for dry throats,

the shoes not yet worn,
the new crisp raincoat,
the bottled water,
the smiling tour guides,

the crisp white sheets,
the mosquito net which carefully
embraces your evening bed,
and the way your loved one
kisses you good night
under effervescent stars
and the Milky Way

which we can almost touch.

King Pride

Just look how we depend upon
one another, as you proudly
exit this dense yet lonely jungle
sleeking single file,
stomachs full of antelope carcass
rolled flat under our jeep.

It hurts to see you devour,
but really I understand
in this world where
survival whispers signs
of death and hints
at new lives behind the bushes
while you nurse your precious newborn cubs.

Your Camera

dedicated to "RMR"

Each time you lean
your twenty-five-year-old self
outside our safari jeep, camera lens

extended beyond its borders,
I think of your grandfather
who did the same on our family excursions

across both water and land—
his private journeys through view-finders,
the naked eye only a desperate alternative.

Captured memories then carefully centered
between photo binders for safekeeping.
This many years later, I now understand

their significance—snapshots
of his early years were swallowed by
the Nazis, leaving only

mental memories meshed
into the backpacks of future generations
and on the film of his mental camera.

In the end, we have grandpa
to thank for your passion
for the widest view-finder known.

Lost

In a small aircraft,
we, the safari-garbed Americans,
glide high above the plains
seated on a plane barely fitting six.

From the tear on my father's face
to the surge of fear in myself,
I glanced down at my recent test results
and understood life's uncertainties.

We are so far from our home, so lost
in this continent as I reflect
on how home is where
my heart and his soul lurk.

I never fully believed
life's uncertainty
until I planted my own two feet
onto this African soil—

the fears amass where the only givens
are the daily sunrises and sunsets,
where survival is everyone's name.
Nobody knows where

the next day's food will reside.
Neither daylight nor darkness
offers solace for our souls. What clothes
to throw onto our sweaty backs?

Our Mission

Each day at the crack of five
we mount the open jeep,
wheels large enough to swim a deep stream.

The dirt road leads us to the eternal hunt
for cryptic animals. Our leader, called 'Master,'
is the spotter seated high on the front seat,

a twenty-year-old African powered by bliss-
ful love of jungle and its inhabitants. He
clenches a spotlight, his lifeline

to the fauna, rotates
it left to right, right to left,
sweeping terrains for frozen eyes

or a stalled four-legged friend.
He has earned his name from years
of practice here in the jungle where nothing

matters except the scent
of life and death.
This voyage relaxes us—no cell

phone tones or computer hums,
nor doorbell rings or kid thumps—
just freedom's knock on the door

of our minds inside this safari silence
in a world of untapped wonders
all starting first thing in the morning.

Creatures

Amidst this African terrain,
after staff return to shared cabins,
I hear unrecognizable sounds
of animals singing
elusive evening melodies.

I imagine them lined up one by one,
just outside our tent's front door,
scanning for body-part treats, as I stroll
into the shower alongside
herds of crawling insects.

While washing my left armpit
I decide it's better to ignore
what scares me and paddle
into the night of passions.
I remove the portable Scrabble

inside the netted bed to choose
surprise letters from a shredded bag.
I create familiar words, a reminder
of our life back in America while
a spider surmounts what seems to him

a hairy Mt. Everest, but in reality,
is only my daughter's unshaven leg
which sings a blissful song
free of razor burn.

Their Flu

After the safari
and saturated in the wonder
of wild-running animals,
our family pulls for a tribe visit—
a little fenced-in house perched

on the side of a vacant road,
especially erected for visitors.
Greeted by the warm guide Edna,
we are pulled into her roadside model home
to watch jaded older ladies

glued to their corners, each wrinkle
a sign of buried burdens,
weaving their lives into baskets,
while the young in the distance
pluck roots from herbs,

as men sit in their designated doorways
to craft furniture and musical instruments.
The sun burrows its warmth into my
pith helmet, a relic from the airport gift shop.
Not real, but good enough.

I smell disease here and Edna talks of malaria
as I ask if my kids swallowed
their daily malaria pills
while she stops on the gravel driveway,
turns to me with her wide, radiant smile

and six-foot frame, and aloofly says,
"Oh yeah, I get it every year,"
in the same way
we Westerners
might be struck with the common cold.

IV. Zimbabwe

I'm Wondering

what happened
to the old man at the window
whispering to the clerk at the
bustling Zimbabwe border beside
the sign warning of cholera and HIV

near the condoms in their torn box,
as he pushes his cane closer
to the window ledge begging
for entrance into the country
where his delirious 100-year-old wife

lies in some clinic bed calling
his name, and all he has in his pocket
is one dollar, as the clerk leans closer
and with an impatient tone
yells that he needs nineteen more.

I think about what the Dalai Lama
might have done right then and there,
and to emulate, I reach into my muddy
safari pocket and hand the old guy
the only twenty I have and wish him

a good day or however many more
he might be blessed with
before his God calls him to the gates
of his own private heaven which
one day he'll call home, hopefully
right alongside his wife.

Camp Lessons

We gather in a circle
on the meeting room sofa

inaccessible to other visitors
and are handed a paper stack—

the rules to this new camp
highlighted by the rehashed warning

not to venture out alone at night.

But when my middle daughter's
phone shatters to the floor

after the sun sets below its horizon
and the scorpion lands

to visit a chunk of her toe,
she does something she swore

she would never do. She grabs
the big blow horn from the corner of her tent

and presses down as hard
as she can and thanks to her daily workouts

the elephants are even impressed,
although they must still wonder

what could be happening
in tent number 1051.

Hippos

You might have only seen a hippo
in your favorite neighborhood zoo
and you might have thought him

harmless, sunbathing in his spot,
bobbing up and down in frigid waters
while air blew from his cryptic orifices.

It is different in Africa—they do not reach
for the air because their territory is their master.
They are herbivores unless you anger them;

then they will dunk you to the bottom
of their waterway never to be kissed again.
Our jeep arrived at sunset

at the edge of their swamp
as their big papa sat and stared
deep into our foreign eyes, long enough

to bring ten more in his company,
as if this army could infiltrate
our veins with fear. They sat proudly

slithered with hissing sounds
and a display of the goings on
inside their mouths, teeth which

I would rather have seen in the zoo cabinet
than jammed into my flesh.
Under my breath, but loud enough

for each to hear, I said "You win"
and shivered as our jeep approached
to test the water they know best.

The Speckled One

Amidst the jungle
and animals
I saw a giraffe
all beige
with black speckles
in a wide field
grazing
relaxed
unmoved
by the spinning wheels
bell dongs
and human chatter
along the safari path.

Baobab Trees and Hyenas

If you stumble upon the baobab,
chances are you will not stop
staring because it looks
as if someone stuck
it into the ground upside down,

and you will learn how
in the beginning each animal
was given a tree to plant

and the hyena chose this one,
which he mistakenly
planted upside down,
and if you open your ears
echoes of older souls will whisper

that Africans do not much like the hyena
and if you take a moment to watch one,
you will understand why, as it

sleeks around sniffing carcasses.
If you stop and stare long enough
at the young baobab,
you will notice
how it resembles God's thumb

and his way to ward off
evil spirits—an appendage
I wish I had right now,

right here in my own
backyard as the full moon
lurks in my own corner
while coyotes howl looking
for my little white dog
which I refuse to trade—
not even for a rare baobab tree.

The Gentlest Animal

has toes even, unlike mine—my second,
larger than the first, which they say

points to creativity—but
the giraffe is much more creative

it seems because of where he reaches
for his sustenance.

Here in Africa I fell in love
with the giraffe and on our

last day, market day,
snatched a wooden purple-spotted one,

standing tall, staring into my green eyes,
to become my single souvenir and carry-on.

Is it their gentleness
or the reminder of my own neck's woes
which draws me to them?

Mischievous Monkeys

This morning as I sat reading my book
inside the empty breakfast tent,
my eyes caught some stirrings
on a buffet of exotic cheeses.

A family of funny monkeys
from a neighboring tree were tempted
by this edible fermentation, as they
sprang themselves onto
the decorated elongated table.

I stood up and tip-toed in their direction.
After another monkey spotted me
and stared deep into my green eyes,
warning me to leave, he tossed

himself onto a nearby branch,
cheese dangling from his primate mouth.
The hostess announced her presence
and clapped them away while another rascal
dropped slippery green grapes to the ground

and scurried up yet another tree.
He glanced back at me like a naughty child
who understands a forehead
written with punishment,

like the one given to my children
during their own mischievous moments.

Here in this African jungle,
I do not want to be a parent—
all I want to do is chuckle
and slowly sip my coffee
and skip along with my day.

The Circle

In the distant field
vultures hover over a mass

and as we slowly approach,
the image falls into focus—one hundred

birds feast on an elephant
carcass, like the hawks back home

do on our cottontails.
They peck inside

the galleys of each
orifice and crevice
of this behemoth beast

nestled in a stench beyond
this poet's description.

My family yearns to linger
and witness the horror, but

I cast my vote to move on.
I do not enjoy witnessing
this innate circle of life.

Let the predators act privately
in the darkness of their night.

Dung Beetles

It is an early Botswana morning
and the dew clings to the mellow marsh.

Through our binoculars
we scan for animals, while our driver

points down to dung beetle tracks.
As a city girl, I see only a bare swamp,

until this round tennis-ball-size
mound of mud transports itself

across a closed concave path.
While my naked eyes morph into magnifiers,

the beetle pushes along, as his female
clings for life onto the perimeter of this ball

of elephant dung once mistaken for mud.
Mr. Dung rolls his straight school ruler's edge line,

and he advances as fast as he can.
As he propels forth his breeding ground,

I wonder what it might look like
if I rolled my king-sized bed up Fifth Avenue

during my own mating season.

Tse Tse Paradise

An early evening game ride
rolls us through high savannah grass,
to where sleeping sickness lurks
and a bug blanket forms
to burrow under
our glistening white skins
coated with toxic repellants
which my doctor says
are better than
the disease they protect against.

We relentlessly duck and swat them away,
those pregnant noiseless flies
smothering us with their bug shower,
my son with a woolen blanket suspended
over his twenty-year-old head,
as we all dart from what could be
the absolutely fatal bite.

Elephant Cluster

It is some day in December
inside a boat on the Zambezi river
with still water and blue sky—

the mood that makes you want to write
but instead, you look up
and twenty elephants

have stolen your attention
on their traipse from jungle to shore.
They tromp down the tangled hill,

a natural parade, not the kind
taught at the end of a leather strap.
Babies and mothers march in single file,

trunks lifted to the heavens,
and then thrust down into the river,
to slurp nature's wine

in their very own crystal.
I remember the picture of Babar
hanging on my son's wall

with his baby in Africa
and thoughts rummage through my mind.
I sense the voice of freedom

offering itself and I want
little more than to give it back.
When I step onto

my rich soil of freedom,
I swear never to visit a zoo again.

In Wonder

Today
we saunter to one of the seven
Natural Wonders—

Victoria Falls in Zimbabwe,
where food, water and clothes
are the money the natives speak,
where only twenty percent work,
and eight million each day go to bed hungry
as others rest in the neighbor's trenches.
Sadness drips from unborn eyes
in this country of many such resources
laden with apathetic leaders.

Whilst the other worldly wonders—
Grand Canyon
Great Barrier Reef
Harbour of Rio de Janeiro
Mount Everest
Northern Lights
and Paricutin Volcano

move peacefully into their next daylight.

The Market Visit

Our van parades
into this Victoria Falls market,
met by swarms of vendors
begging for our names and needs.

My son mistakenly announces
he wants a box, and like a torch
of lightning, in half a second
a slew of hungry vendors arrive

to offer more choices
than he can snatch at a glance.
They plea for his quick decision,
a bargain or barter, and he is tempted

by an offer to exchange his hat
for their box, or his soiled gym socks
for their bookends. I lean into the backdrop
and ask myself how they might feed their young.

In haste to gather gifts for friends back home,
we buy elephant hair bracelets,
zebra-patterned materials, bowls and boxes, but
for the vendors—not enough.

We climb into our private van,
as desperate merchants continue to plead,
their wings spread across the van's
roof and windows, pressing their crafts onto us—

one more attempt to feed
their famished families—in this local market.

Poverty

So little sustains
the life
of poverty
sorrowful
dabbled with dirty
water
beside the white
businessman.

No Gala

In this dark jungle
my watch announces
the year's last day.

If we were in America,
we would be stealing
an afternoon nap—

our passport to drinking all night—
but we are in Africa and revels
lurk only in the basins

of our dormant memories.
Times Square sparkles with glitz
and galas fan out across our country

as our moon lingers on the periphery
and the hyena howls the end
of yet another day. Today only marks

one more moment in history
where all that matters is survival,
not measured by how much glitter, green,

Jaguars or mansions spread upon
suburban hills, as money
sleeps in faraway banks

and bureaucrats boast
with petty arguments, and fields
fill with herds, dazzles

and flocks all fight for food.
There are so many different ways
to start and finish the New Year.

The Last Evening of 2008 in Africa

On the edge of our midnight cruise,
while I slide my plastic wine glass
onto the hand-crafted wooden table
in its center, I ponder

my yearly accomplishments,
ups and downs, ins and outs
and hopes for the New Year.
Africa casts a somber perspective

on our sheltered American life,
frivolities and extravagances
amidst the effervescent local smiles.
All our joys are quickly undone and misunderstood—

and my emotions overflow
like the modest champagne
soon to be replenished by dancing servers
and their straw-covered bodies

in this darkness whose midnight
is blacker than their skin.
I miss the ball dropping, but not really
as we place our trust in these people

to know the right moment to celebrate
as they sweat to their Caribbean tunes
in their exotic homemade New Year garb.
Tonight I want to go home.

Departure Morning

As we gather our belongings
hunched over suitcases

set for the trip home, I glance
down at my five pairs of safari shorts,

warm wool socks and rain jackets
and wonder about their future use.

At breakfast we hear our guide
speak of once-a-month ten dollar bus rides

to visit families, and my heart
bleeds into his story

as I realize how there is really little we can do
to redress his life here in Zimbabwe

where houses are vandalized, burned
and run down and where natives

labor long hours for food
or clothing and where currency

holds no meaning.
I march to my tent and grab

the laundry basket hidden beneath my bed
to pile my safari clothes, folded in neat piles.

I tromp up the hill grasping its handles
to tell our guide that my stuff is for his people.

He turns around and hugs me tight
and with a shattered sense of love says,

"You made me a spiritual millionaire!"—
And I feel my blood bubble with joy.

Trip Summary

You can have the Bahamas, Figi, and Belize.
You can have Club Med and Pebble Beach Golf Resort.

Now, the only place that tugs me is a
faraway world with hidden surprises,

where barefoot young pilots
land and take off on short gravel runways

as sweat drips from my brow of curiosity.
So return the fluffy softened towels,

perfumed personally wrapped soaps,
roll-on suitcases and collapsible luggage racks

and take in nature singing at sunrise,
lighting the dance of barefoot smiling maids

lugging buckets of homemade detergents
down long winding wooden paths,

fresh-baked breads and open markets.
They will bestow you with memories

guaranteed to make you weep, even
if you live your time there in unforgettable fear.

About the Author

Diana M. Raab is an award-winning poet, memoirist and registered nurse who teaches in the UCLA Extension Writers' Program and at various conferences around the country.

She is the author of three poetry collections, *My Muse Undresses Me* (2007); *Dear Anaïs: My Life in Poems for You* (2008), winner of The Reader Views Award and an Allbooks Review Editor's Choice Award; and *The Guilt Gene* (2009).

Her poetry and prose have appeared in numerous journals and anthologies including *Rattle, Rosebud, Litchfield Review, Tonopah Review, Writers' Journal, Common Ground Review, The Smoking Poet, A Café in Space, the Toronto Quarterly, Snail Mail Review, New Mirage Journal, Lucidity, Blood and Thunder, Jet Fuel Review,* and *Ascent*.

She's editor of *Writers and Their Notebooks,* winner of a 2011 Eric Hoffer Award and finalist for Best Books (*USA Book News*), and also co-edited (with James Brown) *Writers on the Edge.*

Diana Raab's memoir, *Regina's Closet: Finding My Grandmother's Secret Journal,* won the 2008 National Indie Excellence Award for Memoir and the 2009 Mom's Choice Award for Adult Nonfiction. Her self-help memoir, *Healing With Words: A Writer's Cancer Journey,* won the 2011 Mom's Choice Award for Adult Nonfiction.

For more information, visit her website: www.dianaraab.com.

This book is set in Garamond Premier Pro, which had its genesis in 1988 when type-designer Robert Slimbach visited the Plantin-Moretus Museum in Antwerp, Belgium, to study its collection of Claude Garamond's metal punches and typefaces. During the mid-fifteen hundreds, Garamond—a Parisian punch-cutter—produced a refined array of book types that combined an unprecedented degree of balance and elegance, for centuries standing as the pinnacle of beauty and practicality in type-founding. Slimbach has created an entirely new interpretation based on Garamond's designs and on comparable italics cut by Robert Granjon, Garamond's contemporary.

To order additional copies of this book
or other Antrim House titles, contact the publisher at

Antrim House
21 Goodrich Rd., Simsbury, CT 06070
860.217.0023, AntrimHouse@comcast.net
or the house website (www.AntrimHouseBooks.com).

•

On the house website
are sample poems, upcoming events,
and a "seminar room" featuring supplemental biography,
notes, images, poems, reviews, and
writing suggestions.